S0-AFS-154

DATE DUE			
2-13	Cara D. TJA		22

Holiday Magic Books

Columbus Day

MAGIC

by James W. Baker
pictures by George Overlie

Lerner Publications Company Minneapolis

To magician Lou Osborne and his wife and assistant, Sheri, whose friendship I treasure, and whose creativity in performing and promoting the wonderful world of magic is raising the cause of conjuring to new heights.

Library of Congress Cataloging-in-Publication Data
Baker, James W., 1926-
    Columbus Day magic/by James W. Baker; pictures by George
Overlie.
        p.   cm.—(Holiday magic books)
    Summary: Explains ten magic tricks revolving around a Columbus
Day theme.
    ISBN 0-8225-2237-3 (lib. bdg.)
    1. Tricks—Juvenile literature.   2. Columbus Day—Juvenile
literature. [1. Magic tricks.   2. Columbus Day.]   I. Overlie,
George, ill.   II. Title.   III. Series: Baker, James W., 1926-
Holiday magic books.
GV1548.B3335   1990   89-2681
793.8—dc19   CIP
                                                            AC

Manufactured in the United States of America

1 2 3 4 5 6 7 8 9 10 98 97 96 95 94 93 92 91 90

CONTENTS

6

INTRODUCTION

When Christopher Columbus set sail from Spain in 1492, lots of people thought he was crazy. While most sailors were sailing east to the Orient, Columbus believed he could find an easier way by sailing due west.

Of course, Columbus did not find the western passage to the Orient. But he did astound Europe with his discovery of a "New World" across the Atlantic. Columbus explored the new lands and paved the way for thousands of European explorers and settlers to come after him to the Americas.

You too can set sail for a new world—a world of illusion—with *Columbus Day Magic*. You will astound your friends and have oceans of fun as you discover the secrets and explore the magic of these ten tricks with a Columbus Day theme.

DISCOVERING AMERICA

HOW IT LOOKS

Give your friend 10 index cards, each with the name of a part of the world on it. Then give her instructions for moving the card. She always ends up holding the part of the world discovered by Christopher Columbus — America.

8

You will need 10 index cards, each bearing the name of a part of the world in the time of Columbus, including America.

HOW TO DO IT

1. With all 10 cards facedown, shuffle them thoroughly.
2. Ask your friend to look at the cards and note how far down from the top of the pack is the "America" card.
3. With your friend still holding the cards facedown, have her follow these instructions:
   A. Move five cards, one at a time, from the top to the bottom of the pack.
   B. Have your friend say aloud how far down in the pack the "America" card is. If she says "three," for example, she should move three cards from the top to the bottom of the pack, one at a time.

- A -

move 5 top cards, one at a time, to bottom of deck

5 cards

THREE

- B -

5 cards

move top 3 cards to the bottom of the deck

- C -

1 card

move one more card to the bottom of the deck

10

C. Move one more card from top to bottom.

D. Deal the top card onto the table. Move the next card from the top to the bottom of the pack. Again, deal the top card onto the table and move the next card to the bottom of the pack.

E. Have your friend continue this pattern, dealing, moving, dealing, moving, etc., until your friend has only one card left in her hand. It will always be the "America" card.

deal top card onto the table

move the next card to the bottom of the deck

continue dealing the top card to the table and the next card to the bottom of the deck until one card remains. The card your friend has left will always be the "AMERICA" card

11

HOW IT LOOKS

Lay five index cards—each with the name of a famous explorer written on it—in random order on the table. Ask your friend to concentrate on any one of the five explorers. You write a prediction on a small card and put it in your pocket. Ask your friend to announce the name of the explorer he selected. You then bring the small card out of your pocket and show that you predicted correctly.

12

1. On five index cards, write the names of five famous explorers as shown (**Figure 1**).

figure 1.

2. You will also need five little cards the size of business cards, about 2 x 3 inches (5 x 8 cm). Leave one of these cards blank. On the other four, write the names of Sir Francis Drake, Ferdinand Magellan, Marco Polo, and Amerigo Vespucci (**Figure 2**).

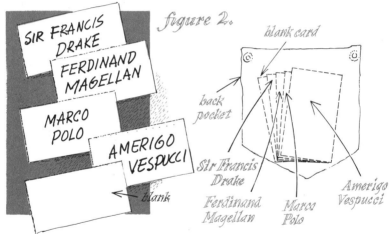

figure 2.

SIR FRANCIS DRAKE

FERDINAND MAGELLAN

MARCO POLO

AMERIGO VESPUCCI

← blank

blank card

back pocket

Sir Francis Drake

Ferdinand Magellan

Marco Polo

Amerigo Vespucci

3. Ahead of time, put all five little cards in your pocket, the blank card closest to your body, and the other four in alphabetical order.

1. After your friend concentrates on one explorer, remove the blank card from your pocket.

2. Without letting your friend see what you are writing, write "Christopher Columbus" on the card. Put the card back in your pocket, again, closest to your body. Be sure to use the same pencil or pen you used to write on the other four small cards.

3. Have your friend announce the name of the explorer he concentrated on.

4. You reach into your pocket and take out the appropriate card. You know which one to bring out because they are in alphabetical order. No one knows that you already had four other prediction cards in your pocket.

THE ROUND EARTH

HOW IT LOOKS

Tell the audience that when Columbus sailed to America he was trying to sail around the earth and prove that the earth is round, not flat. Ask for a volunteer to be "Columbus." Have her follow your directions to make a circle from a flat piece of paper. You point out that even though "Columbus" has made a perfect circle, the paper is still flat. It is not a globe like the earth.

16

HOW TO MAKE IT

For this trick, you will need a piece of paper, a pencil, a pair of scissors, a ruler, and a compass — the type used for drawing circles.

HOW TO DO IT

1. Have "Columbus" use the ruler to draw a quadrilateral—a four-sided figure with straight lines (**Figure 1**). Then have her cut it out.

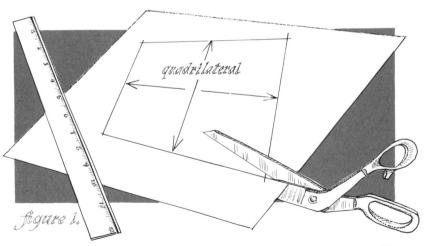

quadrilateral

figure 1.

2. Have her draw an arc — a partial circle — on each corner of the quadrilateral (**Figure 2**) without adjusting the compass. Then have her tear off the corners of the quadrilateral and rearrange them.

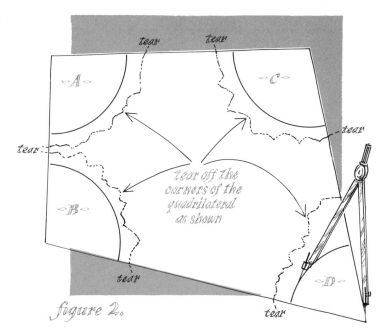

tear   tear

A

C

tear

tear

tear off the corners of the quadrilateral as shown

B

D

tear

figure 2.

tear

3. Even though the four arcs were torn out of a flat piece of paper, they fit together to form a perfect circle (**Figure 3**).

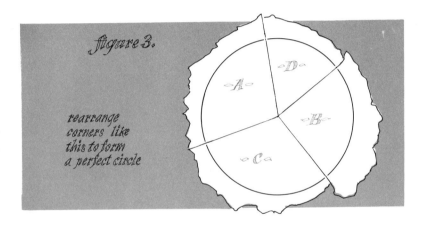

figure 3.

rearrange corners like this to form a perfect circle

Start to congratulate "Columbus" for proving that the earth is round — then stop and look at the paper again. Even though "Columbus" has made a circle, it is still flat, not a globe like the earth. The joke is on Columbus.

HOW IT LOOKS

Ask your friend to shuffle a deck of cards and give the deck back to you. You dribble the cards into a large paper bag, a few at a time. Close the bag and shake it up to mix the cards. Have your friend blindfold you, and while blindfolded, reach into the bag and take out four cards. Ask what year Columbus discovered the New World. When your friend says 1492, drop the four cards on the table. They are a one (ace), a four, a nine, and a two.

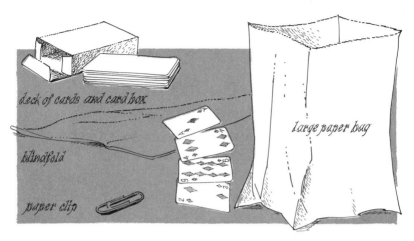

deck of cards and card box

large paper bag

blindfold

paper clip

HOW TO MAKE IT

1. You will need a deck of playing cards, a large paper bag, a blindfold, and a paper clip.
2. Ahead of time, secretly remove an ace, a four, a nine, and a two from the deck.
3. Clip these four cards together with the paper clip and put the clipped pack into the paper bag (**Figure 1**).
4. Put the rest of the cards back in their box.

HOW TO DO IT

1. Follow the steps described in the section on HOW IT LOOKS. When you reach into the paper bag, blindfolded, it is easy to feel the four cards clipped together with the paper clip.

2. Slip the paper clip off, leaving it behind in the bag, and bring out the four cards.

3. Slip off the blindfold, ask your friend what year Columbus discovered the New World, and when he answers, drop the four cards on the table in the proper order: ace, four, nine, and two... 1492.

figure 1.

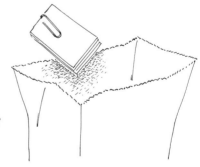

clip together an
ace, a four, a nine
and a two — drop into
a paper bag

put the rest of the cards
into their box

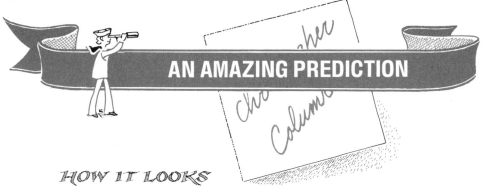

AN AMAZING PREDICTION

HOW IT LOOKS

Show the audience a sealed envelope and tell them there is a prediction inside. Set the envelope in plain view where everyone can see it. Then show the audience a stack of different colored cards with names of explorers, continents, oceans, and seas written on them. Ask a volunteer to mix up the cards and hand them to you behind your back. You turn around and hand the volunteer one yellow card. On it is written "Christopher Columbus." When the sealed envelope is opened, the audience reads your prediction: "Christopher Columbus on a yellow card." Your prediction is correct.

HOW TO MAKE IT

1. Cut out 34 cards, each about two inches (5 cm) square, from five or six different colors of construction paper. Write "Christopher Columbus" on a yellow card and put it in your back pocket.

2. On the other 33 cards, write:

  A. The names of the seven continents: Africa, Antarctica, Asia, Australia, Europe, North America, and South America.

  B. The names of 12 seas: Adriatic, Aegean, Arabian, Baltic, Bering, Black, Caribbean, Caspian, Mediterranean, North, Red, and Yellow.

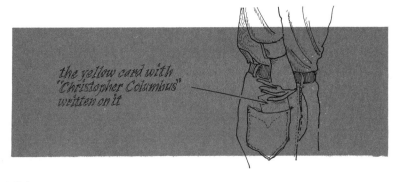

the yellow card with "Christopher Columbus" written on it

C. The names of the five oceans: Antarctic, Arctic, Atlantic, Indian, and Pacific.

D. The names of nine famous explorers: James Cook, Vasco Da Gama, Sir Francis Drake, Erik the Red, Leif Eriksson, Henry Hudson, Ferdinand Magellan, Marco Polo, and Amerigo Vespucci.

3. Write "Christopher Columbus on a yellow card" on a slip of paper and seal it in an envelope.

HOW TO DO IT

1. Show the audience the sealed envelope and tell them you've made a prediction ahead of time.

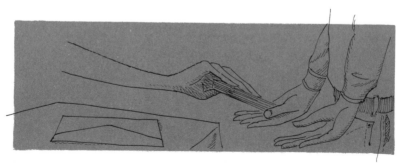

2. Show a volunteer the mixed-up cards of different colors. Tell her the cards have the names of explorers, continents, oceans, and seas on them. Have her mix up the cards even more.

3. Turn around and ask her to hand you the cards behind your back. Then face front again.

4. Pretend to concentrate on what you're doing behind your back. Actually, you reach into your back pocket and take out the yellow card with Christopher Columbus's name on it. The audience will think you took it from the pack.

5. Lay the card on the table and ask the volunteer to open the sealed envelope.

6. Everyone will see that you found the card you predicted ahead of time: "Christopher Columbus on a yellow card."

SANTA MARIA'S WHEEL

HOW IT LOOKS

Tell your friend that right before Columbus was ready to sail to the New World, he discovered that only two of his three ships, the *Nina* and the *Pinta*, had ship's wheels for steering. The *Santa Maria* was missing its wheel. Columbus then called on a magician who, in a matter of seconds, cut out a ship's wheel from a piece of newspaper. You then proceed to do just that.

For this trick, you will need a large, double-page sheet of newspaper, a pencil, and a pair of scissors. Ahead of time, prepare the newspaper as follows:

A. Take the sheet of newspaper and cut it so it is square.

B. Fold corner D up to corner A (**Figure 1**).

C. Fold corner B down to corner C (**Figure 2**).

D. Fold corner AD down to corner CB (**Figure 3**).

E. Fold corner E down, to bring edge EF along edge AF (**Figure 4**). With a pencil, draw faint lines on the paper as shown (**Figure 5**).

cut newspaper into a square

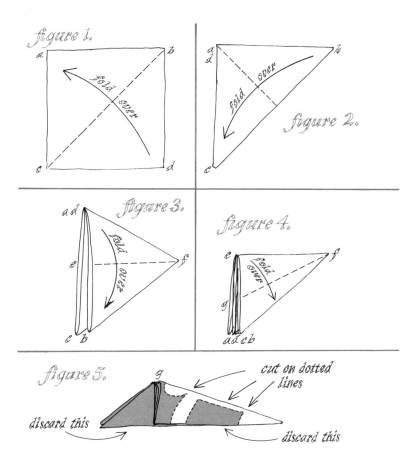

figure 1.

a   b

fold over

c   d

figure 2.

a
d   b

fold over

c

figure 3.

a d   f

e

fold over

c   b

figure 4.

e   f

fold over

g

a d c b

figure 5.

g

cut on dotted lines

discard this

discard this

29

1. Talk about Columbus and the missing ship's wheel as explained in the section on HOW IT LOOKS.
2. Cut the folded paper with scissors along the pencil lines.
3. Open out the paper to show the ship's wheel for the *Santa Maria*.

A STAMP FROM AMERICA

HOW IT LOOKS

Tell your friend that it is a little-known fact that Christopher Columbus wrote a letter and sent it from America. Of course, you say, since no other Europeans knew America existed, he had to use an invisible stamp on his letter. You then show a postage stamp, cover it with a clear drinking glass, add water, put a saucer on top of the glass, and the stamp becomes invisible, just like the one Christopher Columbus used to send a letter from America.

31

For this trick, you will need a postage stamp, a clear drinking glass, some water, and a saucer.

HOW TO DO IT

1. Place the postage stamp faceup on the table.

2. Set the the drinking glass right on top of the postage stamp. Fill the glass with water. Place a saucer on top of the glass. (**Figure 1**).

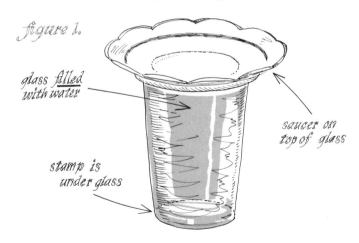

figure 1.

glass filled
with water

saucer on
top of glass

stamp is
under glass

32

3. The stamp will become invisible. You and your friend can look at it from all angles and it will have completely disappeared. Tell your friend he is looking at Christopher Columbus's invisible postage stamp.

4. To make the stamp visible again, simply lift the glass.

lift the glass and the stamp is visible again

COLUMBUS'S THREE SHIPS

HOW IT LOOKS

You show pictures of Christopher Columbus's three ships, the *Nina*, the *Pinta*, and the *Santa Maria*, plus a small portrait of Columbus to the audience. Ask a volunteer from the audience to place the portrait of Columbus on any one of the three ships. Then you show that you predicted ahead of time which ship she would place Columbus's portrait on.

1. On three different colored pieces of construction paper, each about four inches (10 cm) square, draw pictures of Columbus's ships. Label them *Nina*, *Pinta*, and *Santa Maria* (**Figure 1**).

SANTA MARIA   NINA   PINTA

figure 1.

figure 2.

2. Draw a portrait of Christopher Columbus on a round piece of construction paper about two inches (5 cm) across (**Figure 2**). On the back of the portrait, write "You will choose *Nina*. *Chris*"

35

3. On the back of the picture of the *Pinta*, write "Why did you select *Pinta*? *Chris*"

4. On a blank sheet of paper write "I predict you will choose the *Santa Maria*. *Chris*" Put this piece of paper in your pocket.

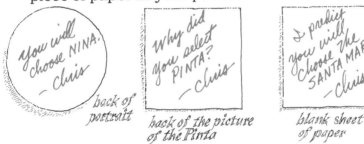

back of portrait

back of the picture of the *Pinta*

blank sheet of paper

HOW TO DO IT

1. Show the audience the pictures of the three ships and the portrait of Columbus. Have a volunteer place the portrait of Columbus on any one of the three ships.

2. When you see which ship she chose, you will know which one of three ways to reveal your prediction:

A. If the volunteer places the portrait on the *Nina*, ask her to turn over Columbus's portrait and read your prediction. Pick up the three ship pictures and place them in your pocket without showing their backs.

B. If the volunteer places the portrait on the *Pinta*, set the portrait aside and ask her to turn over all three ship pictures. She will see that you correctly predicted the *Pinta*.

C. If the volunteer places the portrait on the *Santa Maria*, ask her to reach into your pocket and remove the prediction you made ahead of time which says she will choose the *Santa Maria*. Pick up the pictures of the three ships and the Columbus portrait and put them in your pocket without showing the backs of them to the audience.

You can only perform this trick once for the same audience because you can end it three different ways, depending on which ship is selected.

NINA, PINTA, AND SANTA MARIA

HOW IT LOOKS

Give your friend a piece of paper that has been partially torn into three pieces, each piece bearing the name of one of Christopher Columbus's ships. Challenge your friend to tear the three pieces apart by holding the two outer pieces, one piece in each hand. When she tries to do it, she ends up with two pieces, or ships, in one hand and one in the other. You then proceed to show her how it can be done.

For this trick, you will need a few pieces of paper partially torn into three pieces. On each piece is the name of one of Christopher Columbus's ships: the *Nina*, *Pinta*, and *Santa Maria* (**Figure 1**).

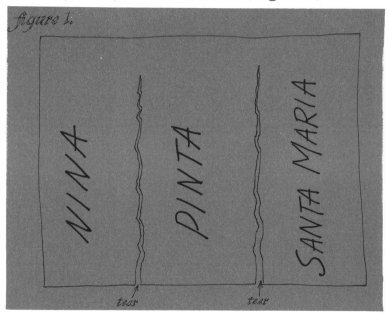

figure 1.

NINA

PINTA

SANTA MARIA

tear   tear

1. No matter how hard your friend tries, she will always end up with two pieces of paper—two ships—in one hand and one piece of paper—one ship—in the other.

2. When you hand the piece of paper to your friend, you might even tell her something like, "You must not touch the middle piece with your hands."

3. Using another sheet of paper prepared the same way, you separate the three pieces—three ships—into three pieces. The secret is that you hold the middle piece of paper in your mouth while pulling on the two outer pieces (**Figure 2**).

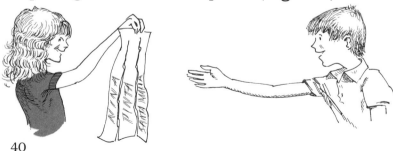

figure 2.

41

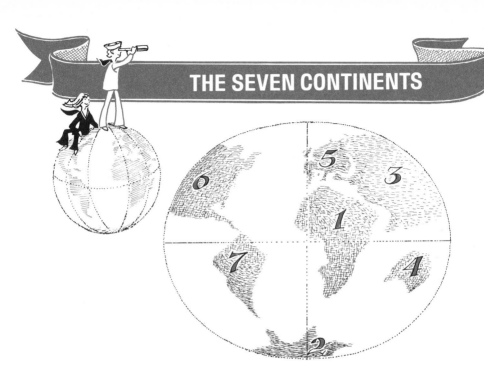

THE SEVEN CONTINENTS

HOW IT LOOKS

You tell your friend about Christopher Columbus sailing west from Europe and how he discovered America instead of a new route to China and Japan. Point out that there are seven continents in the world and hand your friend seven index cards, each bearing the name of a different continent. Have him mix up the cards and hand them to you behind your back. Then face your friend and tell him that you can tell one continent from another strictly by feel. Ask him to name the continents in any order. As he does this, you hand him — one at a time — the card with the continent as he names it.

two identical sets of index cards

HOW TO MAKE IT

1. For this trick, you will need 14 identical index cards.

2. Type the names of the seven continents on seven of the cards, one continent per card: Africa, Antarctica, Asia, Australia, Europe, North America, and South America.

3. Make a duplicate set of the seven cards. Be careful to type the names of the continents in the same place, near the middle, on both sets of cards.

4. Before you begin, secretly put one set of index cards in your back pocket. They should be in alphabetical order from your body outwards. No one knows about this set of cards but you.

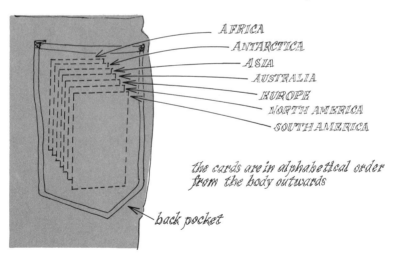

AFRICA
ANTARCTICA
ASIA
AUSTRALIA
EUROPE
NORTH AMERICA
SOUTH AMERICA

the cards are in alphabetical order from the body outwards

back pocket

1. As you talk about Christopher Columbus and the seven continents in the world, you hand out the seven index cards. Have your friend mix up the cards and hand them to you behind your back.

2. As you turn back around to face your friend, you place the mixed-up cards in one back pocket and take out the duplicate set — in alphabetical order—from the other back pocket. Keep the cards behind your back.

3. It is easy for you to hand your friend the cards in the order he calls for them because you know that the Africa card is first, the Antarctica card is second, the Asia card is third, and so forth.

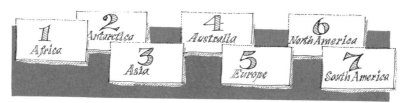

45

TRICKS FOR BETTER MAGIC

Here are some simple rules you should keep in mind while learning to perform the tricks in this book.

1. Read the entire trick several times until you thoroughly understand it.
2. Practice the trick alone or in front of a mirror until you feel comfortable doing the trick, then present it to an audience.
3. Learn to perform one trick perfectly before moving on to another trick. It is better to perform one trick well than a half dozen poorly.
4. Work on your "presentation." Make up special "patter" (what you say while doing a trick) that is funny and entertaining. Even the simplest trick becomes magical when it is properly presented.
5. Choose tricks that suit you and your personality. Some tricks will work better for you than others.

Stick with these. *Every* trick is not meant to be performed by *every* magician.

6. Feel free to experiment and change a trick to suit you and your unique personality so that you are more comfortable presenting it.

7. Never reveal the secret of the trick. Your audience will respect you much more if you do not explain the trick. When asked how you did a trick, simply say "by magic."

8. Never repeat a trick for the same audience. If you do, you will have lost the element of surprise and your audience will probably figure out how you did it the second time around.

9. Take your magic seriously, but not yourself. Have fun with magic and your audience will have fun along with you.

ABOUT THE AUTHOR

James W. Baker, a magician for over 30 years, has performed as "Mister Mystic" in hospitals, orphanages, and schools around the world. He is a member of the International Brotherhood of Magicians and the Society of American Magicians, and is author of *Illusions Illustrated*, a magic book for young performers.

From 1951 to 1963, Baker was a reporter for *The Richmond (VA) News Leader*. From 1963 to 1983, he was an editor with the U.S. Information Agency, living in Washington, D.C., India, Turkey, Pakistan, the Philippines, and Tunisia, and traveling in 50 other countries. Today Baker and his wife, Elaine, live in Williamsburg, Virginia, where he performs magic and writes for the local newspaper, *The Virginia Gazette*.

ABOUT THE ARTIST

George Overlie is a talented artist who has illustrated numerous books. Born in the small town of Rose Creek, Minnesota, Overlie graduated from the New York Phoenix School of Design and began his career as a layout artist. He soon turned to book illustration and proved his skill and versatility in this demanding field. For Overlie, fantasy, illusion, and magic are all facets of illustration and have made doing the Holiday Magic books a real delight.